Visit the author's website at www.coachucation.com.

Featured Artist Illustration © 2020 Leslie Gerhart
and Interior Design by Marcia Schabel

ISBN 9781676315643 (Paperback Edition)

For all of our children and all of ourselves

For ages 9-99 & all the numbers before & after

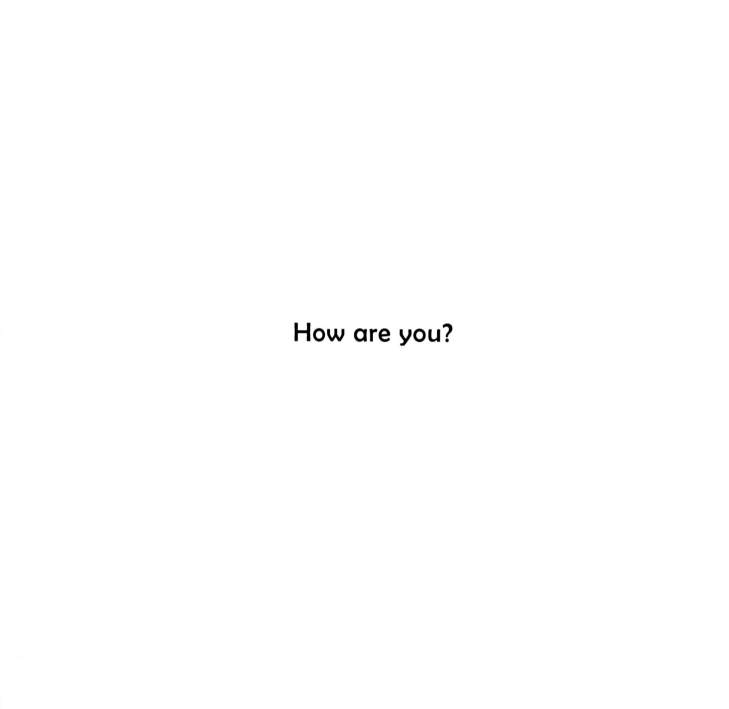

How are you?

You are...

Yearning

Growing Daring

Unique

Transformative

Spacious

Grateful

Trustworthy

Amazing

Intelligent

Lovable

OMG

Radiant

Kind

Resilient

Joyful

Shining

Easeful

Knowledgeable

Forgiving

Noticed

eXtraordinary

Vulnerable

Heartfelt

Talented

Present

Memorable

Brave

Caring

eXpressive

Zany

Bold

Quirky

Worthy

Dreaming

Peaceful

Vibrant

Abundant

"Yeah, but..." you start to say.

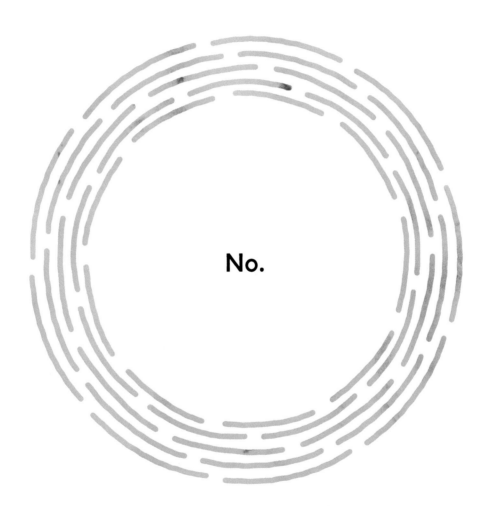

No.

The ocean's waves breathe in and out when you do.
Because...you matter.

The sunflower lifts through its stalk and
shows its face to the sky with pride.
Because...you matter.

The wind calls to you and moves with you.
Because...you matter.

The fog crawls along the earth and hides in plain sight.
Because...you matter.

The sun rises and sets with you.
Because...you matter.

The weeds transform into wild gardens.
Because...you matter.

The sand clings to you.
Because...you matter.

The clouds create shade and pictures for you.
Because...you matter.

The shadows follow you and want to play.
Because...you matter.

The river curves and bends to find you.
Because...you matter.

The trees stretch toward you and dance.
Because...you matter.

The moon explores its phases and shines bright.
Because...you matter.

The mountain shares its rock with you.
Because...you matter.

The stars twinkle for you.
Because...you matter.

You are...

Yearning

Growing

Unique

Daring

Transformative

Grateful Spacious

Lovable

Trustworthy

Abundant

Amazing

LOMG

Radiant

Kind

Intelligent

Easeful

Knowledgeable

Resilient

Joyful

Shining

Forgiving

Noticed

eXtraordinary

Vulnerable

Heartfelt

Present

Memorable

Talented

Caring

eXpressive

Zany

Brave

Bold

Quirky

Worthy

Dreaming

Peaceful

Vibrant

Yes.

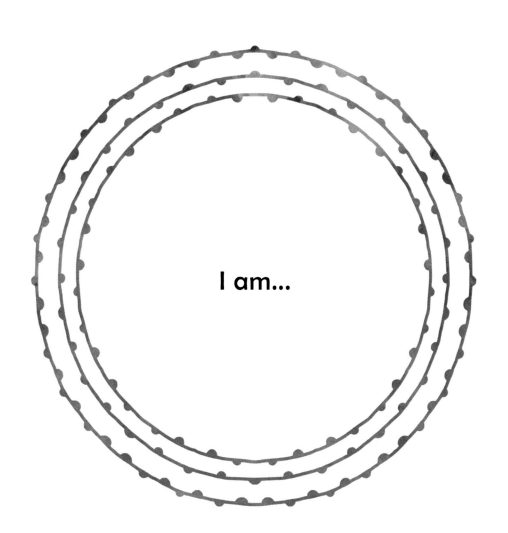

I am...

Pause. Breathe. Notice. Allow.

Because...you matter.

"Am I the center of the Universe?" you ask.

You are someone's center.

Because...You Matter

The ocean's waves breathe in and out when you do.
Because...you matter.

The sunflower lifts through its stalk and shows its face to the sky with pride.
Because...you matter.

The wind calls to you and moves with you.
Because...you matter.

The fog crawls along the earth and hides in plain sight.
Because...you matter.

The sun rises and sets with you.
Because...you matter.

The weeds transform into wild gardens.
Because...you matter.

The sand clings to you.
Because...you matter.

The clouds create shade and pictures for you.
Because...you matter.

The shadows follow you and want to play.
Because...you matter.

The river curves and bends to find you.
Because...you matter.

The trees stretch toward you and dance.
Because...you matter.

The moon explores its phases and shines bright.
Because...you matter.

The mountain shares its rock with you.
Because...you matter.

The stars twinkle for you.
Because...you matter.

About the Author

Suzie is a public school educator, yoga teacher, founder of Coachucation™, a burnout prevention strategist, and the host of the Keep Your Candle Lit podcast. When she isn't doing those things, she can be found with her nose in a book, petting her cats, or hanging out in nature. Suzie hopes that readers of all ages can connect with the message of this book as well as be inspired to spend time in nature. You can connect with Suzie on Instagram @coachucation or by visiting her website coachucation.com.

About the Artist

Leslie is an artist in various mediums: painter, sculptor, mosiacs, jewelry and so much more. When she isn't creating, she is the proud mom of her son Layne, three chickens and a chameleon. One of her favorite things is to reach and meaningfully connect with people through her art. You can connect with Leslie on Instagram @glossystonesart.

About the Designer

Marcia is an intuitive brand designer committed to raising your vibration. When she isn't being creative helping others build soul aligned lives and businesses, she is with her family and 2 mini Goldendoodle pups on an adventure. Each moment in life is a gift to explore, grow, dream, and most importantly, have fun! You can connect with Marcia on Instagram @marcia.schabel or at marciaschabel.com.

Made in the USA
Middletown, DE
16 May 2020